KU-201-738

OUR FAMILY HISTORY

Tracing the story of our life

CONTENTS

How to Use this Book

'Our Family History' has been designed to make it easy to gather together the stories and memories of your family during the past 150 years.

The book is in two parts. Pages 6 to 47 enquire about all your principle relations, asking simple questions. In answering them, you will be writing about the main aspects of your family's life. A few pages may not be immediately relevant to you (you may not have grandchildren, for example), but most of these will probably come into their own in due course.

The second part of the book gives a fascinating visual impression of these 150 years, with photographs of numerous contemporary items from different periods, and pages for you to place the family's story in context.

In the middle of the book, between the two main parts, you will find a simple Family Tree (pages 48 to 51). On the first two pages you can fill in the names of your forebears and on the next two your own and those of subsequent generations. In completing the names of earlier generations you will probably find it easier to trace through from right to left, starting with your parents and going backwards to your grandparents, and so on.

Throughout the book, there are plenty of spaces for photographs, but of course these can also be used for letters, cuttings from magazines and newspapers, or other mementoes.

It is hoped that whoever owns this book will enjoy completing it and creating something quite unique. It is certain to be treasured well into the twenty-first century.

THE PUBLISHERS

$\mathscr{A}$CKNOWLEDGEMENTS

The great majority of the illustrations and items reproduced in this book are from the Robert Opie Collection in Gloucester Docks, Gloucestershire. Mr Opie has given considerable help in the compilation and preparation of this book and we are most grateful to him.

$\mathscr{O}$THER $\mathscr{S}$OURCES OF $\mathscr{H}$ELP

If you want to delve more deeply into your family's history but are not sure how to set about it, you may wish to consult some of the books and magazines designed to help. Those listed below are just a small selection of the many easily obtainable.

"The Family Historian's Enquire Within" by Pauline Saul. The Federation of Family History Societies 1995. ISBN 187 209 483X.

"The Family Tree Detective" by Colin D. Rogers. Manchester University Press 1986. ISBN 0 7190 1846 3.

"The Oxford Guide to Family History" by David Hay. Oxford University Press 1993. ISBN 0 1986 91777.

Family History Monthly. Diamond Publishing Group Ltd., 45 St Mary's Road, London W5 5RQ.

Family Tree Magazine. J.M. and M. Armstrong & Partners, 6 Great Whyte Ramsey, Huntingdon, Cambridgeshire, PE17 1HL.

PEOPLE TO CONTACT

You may wish to get in touch with close acquaintances and relatives to ask them about their memories and impressions of different periods. You could make a list below of all the people you would like to contact.

NAME	ADDRESS AND TELEPHONE NUMBER	✓

GREAT-GRANDPARENTS

Your Father's Father's Parents

YOUR GREAT-GRANDFATHER

Name ....

Date of Birth ....

Place ....

YOUR GREAT-GRANDMOTHER

Maiden Name ....

Date of Birth ....

Place ....

Do you know where they went to school? How did they earn their living?

....

....

....

....

When and where did they marry? Where did they live for most of their lives? Did either of them serve in any major war?

....

....

....

....

Did you ever meet them? What are your recollections of them? What have others told you about them?

....

....

....

....

....

GREAT-GRANDPARENTS

Your Father's Mother's Parents

YOUR GREAT-GRANDFATHER

Name ....

Date of Birth ....

Place ....

YOUR GREAT-GRANDMOTHER

Maiden Name ....

Date of Birth ....

Place ....

Do you know where they went to school? How did they earn their living?

....

....

....

....

When and where did they marry? Where did they live for most of their lives? Did either of them serve in any major war?

....

....

....

....

Did you ever meet them? What are your recollections of them? What have others told you about them?

....

....

....

....

GREAT-GRANDPARENTS

Your Mother's Father's Parents

YOUR GREAT-GRANDFATHER

Name ....

Date of Birth ....

Place ....

YOUR GREAT-GRANDMOTHER

Maiden Name ....

Date of Birth ....

Place ....

Do you know where they went to school? How did they earn their living?

....

....

....

....

When and where did they marry? Where did they live for most of their lives? Did either of them serve in any major war?

....

....

....

....

Did you ever meet them? What are your recollections of them? What have others told you about them?

....

....

....

....

....

....

GREAT-GRANDPARENTS

Your Mother's Mother's Parents

YOUR GREAT-GRANDFATHER

Name ....

Date of Birth ....

Place ....

YOUR GREAT-GRANDMOTHER

Maiden Name ....

Date of Birth ....

Place ....

Do you know where they went to school? How did they earn their living?

....

....

....

....

When and where did they marry? Where did they live for most of their lives? Did either of them serve in any major war?

....

....

....

....

Did you ever meet them? What are your recollections of them? What have others told you about them?

....

....

....

....

GRANDPARENTS

Your Father's Parents

YOUR GRANDFATHER

Name .... Date of Birth .... Place ....

Where did he go to school? What do you know about his early life?

....

....

....

How old was he when he left school? What did he do during his working life? Did he serve in the armed forces for a period?

....

....

....

Can you describe his appearance? What do you recall most vividly about him? What were his greatest interests?

....

....

....

....

....

....

PHOTOGRAPH

GRANDPARENTS

Your Father's Parents

YOUR GRANDMOTHER

Maiden Name .... Date of Birth .... Place ....

Where did she go to school? What were her favourite subjects? Did she go on to any further training or education after she left school? Did she go out to work?

....

....

....

How did she meet your father's father? When and where did they marry? Where did they live when they were first married? How old were they when their first child was born?

....

....

....

....

....

Did you ever meet her? What do you remember most about her?

....

....

....

....

....

GRANDPARENTS

Your Mother's Parents

YOUR GRANDFATHER

Name .... Date of Birth .... Place ....

Where did he go to school? What do you know about his early life?

....

....

....

....

How old was he when he left school? What did he do during his working life? Did he serve in the armed forces for a period?

....

....

....

....

....

....

Can you describe his appearance? What do you recall most vividly about him? What were his greatest interests?

....

....

....

....

....

....

GRANDPARENTS

Your Mother's Parents

YOUR GRANDMOTHER

Maiden Name .... Date of Birth .... Place ....

Where did she go to school? What were her favourite subjects? Did she go on to any further training or education after she left school? Did she go out to work?

....

....

....

How did she meet your mother's father? When and where did they marry? Where did they live when they were first married? How old were they when their first child was born?

....

....

....

....

Did you ever meet her? What do you remember most about her?

....

....

....

....

....

PHOTOGRAPH

GREAT-UNCLES AND GREAT-AUNTS

On Your Father's Side

YOUR GRANDFATHER'S BROTHERS AND SISTERS

NAME	DATE OF BIRTH	PLACE

What were the significant events in their lives? Did they marry and have families? Did any of them emigrate? What family stories are told about them? What are your own memories of them?

PHOTOGRAPH

Great-Uncles and Great-Aunts

On Your Father's Side

Your Grandmother's Brothers and Sisters

NAME	DATE OF BIRTH	PLACE

What were the significant events in their lives? Did they marry and have families? Did any of them emigrate? What family stories are told about them? What are your own memories of them?

GREAT-UNCLES AND GREAT-AUNTS

On Your Mother's Side

YOUR GRANDFATHER'S BROTHERS AND SISTERS

NAME	DATE OF BIRTH	PLACE

What were the significant events in their lives? Did they marry and have families? Did any of them emigrate? What family stories are told about them? What are your own memories of them?

PHOTOGRAPH

GREAT-UNCLES AND GREAT-AUNTS

On Your Mother's Side

YOUR GRANDMOTHER'S BROTHERS AND SISTERS

NAME	DATE OF BIRTH	PLACE

What were the significant events in their lives? Did they marry and have families? Did any of them emigrate? What family stories are told about them? What are your own memories of them?

$\mathcal{P}$ARENTS

$\mathcal{Y}$OUR $\mathcal{F}$ATHER

Name .... Date of Birth .... Place ....

$\mathbb{W}$here did he go to school? $\mathbb{W}$hat did he enjoy most about his school years? $\mathbb{W}$hat did he and his school

friends do in their free time?

....

....

....

$\mathbb{W}$here did his family live? $\mathbb{W}$here did they go on holiday?

....

....

....

....

....

$\mathcal{P}$HOTOGRAPH

$\mathbb{D}$id he go on to further education? $\mathbb{I}$f so, where did

he go and what did he study?

....

....

....

....

....

$\mathcal{P}$ARENTS

$\mathbb{W}$hat was his first job? $\mathbb{W}$hat occupation did he follow for most of his life? $\mathbb{D}$id he ever serve in the armed forces? $\mathbb{H}$ow did he spend his spare time?

....

....

....

....

....

....

....

....

$\mathbb{W}$hen and where did he meet your mother? $\mathbb{H}$ow long were they going out together before they married? $\mathbb{W}$here was their first home together?

....

....

....

....

....

....

$\mathbb{W}$hat are your happiest childhood memories of him? $\mathbb{W}$hat do you remember best about him?

....

....

....

....

....

PARENTS

YOUR MOTHER

Maiden Name .... Date of Birth .... Place ....

Where did she go to school? What subjects did she do best at? What sports did she enjoy most?

....
....
....
....
....
....

Where did her family live when she was young? Where did they go on holiday? What was the most interesting thing that happended to her as a girl?

....
....
....
....
....
....

What did she do after leaving school? Did she go to university or college?

....
....
....
....

$\mathscr{P}$ARENTS

$\mathbb{W}$hat was her first job? $\mathbb{H}$ow much did she earn? $\mathbb{W}$hat did she enjoy doing in her spare time?

....

....

....

....

....

$\mathbb{H}$ow old was she when she became a mother? $\mathbb{W}$hat are your earliest memories of her?

....

....

....

....

....

....

$\mathbb{W}$hat is the best piece of advice she ever gave you?

....

....

....

....

....

....

....

....

$\mathscr{P}$HOTOGRAPH

Uncles and Aunts

On Your Father's Side

Your Father's Brothers and Sisters

NAME	DATE OF BIRTH	PLACE

Were they close as a family? Do they still keep in touch with one another?

....

....

....

Did you see much of them when you were young? What are your most vivid memories of them?

....

....

....

....

....

What occupations did they follow? Are there any interesting or funny stories about them?

....

....

....

....

....

Uncles and Aunts

On Your Mother's Side

Your Mother's Brothers and Sisters

NAME	DATE OF BIRTH	PLACE

Were they close as a family? Do they still keep in touch with one another?

Did you see much of them when you were young? What are your most vivid memories of them?

What occupations did they follow? Are there any interesting or funny stories about them?

Your Cousins

On Your Father's Side

COUSIN'S NAME	YOUR AUNT'S NAME	YOUR UNCLE'S NAME	BORN ON

Did you see much of each other when you were young? What do you remember about them?

What have been the notable events in their lives so far? Do you keep in touch with any of them? What are they doing now?

Have there been any special occasions when you have all been together?

YOUR COUSINS

On Your Mother's Side

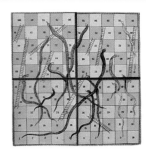

COUSIN'S NAME	YOUR AUNT'S NAME	YOUR UNCLE'S NAME	BORN ON

Did you see much of each other when you were young? What do you remember about them?

What have been the notable events in their lives so far? Do you keep in touch with any of them? What are they doing now?

Have there been any special occasions when you have all been together?

ABOUT YOURSELF

Name .... Date of Birth ....

Place .... Weight at Birth .... Time ....

Why did your parents choose your first name?

....

....

....

Where did you live as a child? Did you move home when you were young?

....

....

....

....

....

....

....

Which schools did you go to? Do you remember any of your teachers? What did you enjoy most at school? Which were your best subjects?

....

....

....

....

....

....

PHOTOGRAPHS

Did you go to college or university? **W**hat was your first job? **H**ow much were you paid?

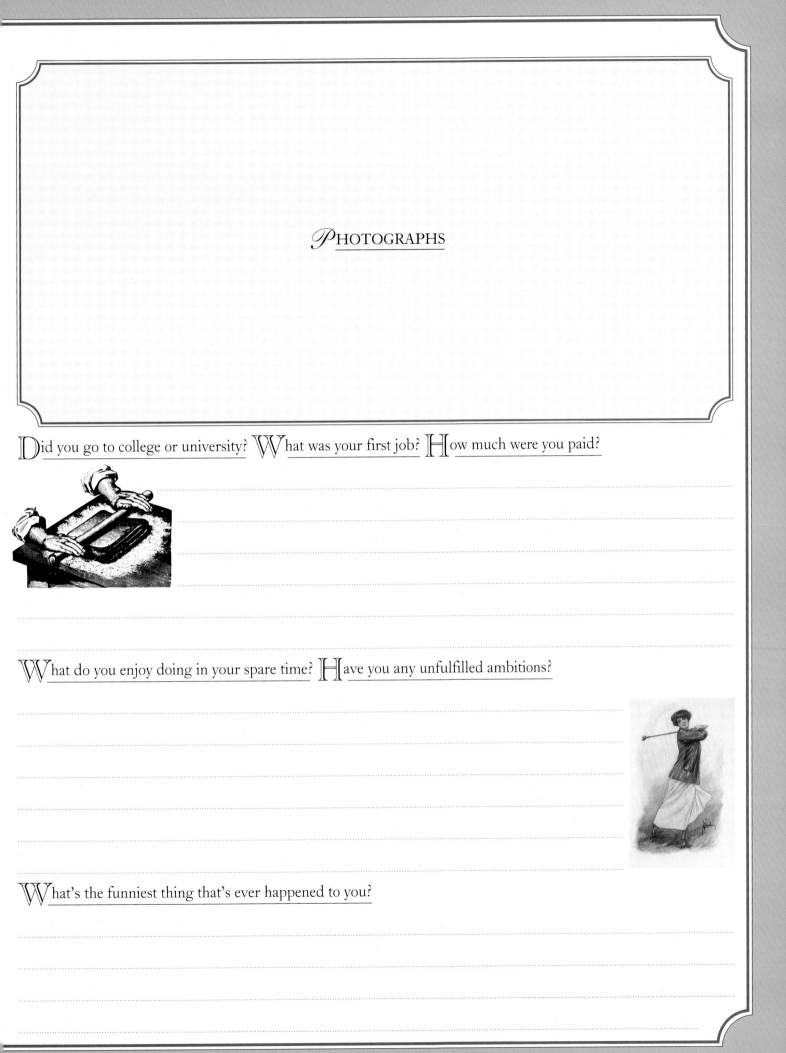

What do you enjoy doing in your spare time? **H**ave you any unfulfilled ambitions?

What's the funniest thing that's ever happened to you?

Your Brothers and Sisters

NAME	DATE OF BIRTH	PLACE

Did you all go to the same schools?

Were there any particular games you used to play together when you were young? Did you have nick-names for one another? What are the happiest memories you have of your early life together?

Which of you was most often in trouble and what for? Did you all enjoy good health?

Your Brothers and Sisters

Have any of them married? If so, when, where and to whom?

NAME	MARRIED	PLACE	DATE

What are they doing now?

....

....

....

....

What are the most interesting or unusual things that have happened to them?

....

....

....

....

....

....

....

....

PHOTOGRAPH

Your Spouse

Name .... Date of Birth ....

Place .... Weight at Birth .... Time ....

When and how did you meet? Were your backgrounds and interests similar?

....

....

....

....

Where did you first go out to together by yourselves, and what did you do?

....

....

....

....

Photograph

How long had you been going out together before you became engaged?

....

....

....

Your Spouse

When and where were you married? Who were the best man and the bridesmaids? What do you remember most about your wedding?

Did you have a honeymoon? If so, where did you go? How did you choose where to live? What was your first home like?

How much did you have to live on when you were first married? What were your first years together like?

$\mathscr{Y}$OUR $\mathscr{P}$ARENTS-IN-LAW

$\mathscr{Y}$OUR $\mathscr{F}$ATHER-IN-LAW

Name ....

Date of Birth ....

Place ....

$\mathscr{Y}$OUR $\mathscr{M}$OTHER-IN-LAW

Maiden Name ....

Date of Birth ....

Place ....

$\mathscr{W}$hen did you first meet your parents-in-law? $\mathscr{W}$here were they living? $\mathscr{W}$hat were their occupations?

....

....

....

$\mathscr{W}$here do they live now? $\mathscr{H}$ow often do you see them? $\mathscr{W}$hat do you know about their early life together?

....

....

....

....

$\mathscr{Y}$OUR $\mathscr{S}$POUSE'S $\mathscr{G}$RANDPARENTS

Father-in-law's Father .... Date of Birth ....

Father-in-law's Mother .... Date of Birth ....

Mother-in-law's Father .... Date of Birth ....

Mother-in-law's Mother .... Date of Birth ....

$\mathscr{H}$ave you ever met your spouse's grandparents? $\mathscr{D}$o you remember when and where?

....

....

....

Your Parents-in-Law

Your Spouse's Uncles and Aunts

NAME	BROTHER/SISTER OF	DATE OF BIRTH

Do any of them live close by? Do the two sides of your family ever meet?

Your Spouse's Cousins

COUSIN'S NAME	CHILD OF/AND	DATE OF BIRTH

Was your spouse particularly close to any of them as a child?

YOUR SPOUSE'S BROTHERS AND SISTERS

NAME	DATE OF BIRTH	PLACE

Where did the family live when they were growing up? Did they all get on well together?

What stories do your parents-in-law tell about their children when they were young?

Did they go on to further education after school?

Your Spouse's Brothers and Sisters

Have any of them married? If so, when, where and to whom?

NAME	MARRIED	PLACE	DATE

What have been their occupations and jobs?

What are the most interesting or unusual things that have happened to them?

PHOTOGRAPH

Your Children

NAME	DATE OF BIRTH	PLACE	TIME	WEIGHT

Why did you choose the names you gave them?

Who in the family do they most look like?

How old were they when they learned to crawl, walk, eat with a spoon, write their name, ride a bike . . . ?

Your Children

What is the most endearing characteristic of each of them?

....

....

....

Do they all get on well together?

....

....

....

What do you think has, for each of them, been the single most important event in their life?

....

....

....

....

Photographs

$\mathcal{N}$EPHEWS AND $\mathcal{N}$IECES

$\mathcal{Y}$OUR $\mathcal{B}$ROTHERS' AND $\mathcal{S}$ISTERS' $\mathcal{C}$HILDREN

NAME	CHILD OF/AND	DATE OF BIRTH

$\mathcal{D}$o you remember any incidents from their early childhood? $\mathcal{W}$hat are they doing at this stage of their lives?

....

....

....

....

....

$\mathcal{H}$as there ever been an occasion when they and all your children have been together at the same time?

....

....

....

....

....

....

....

$\mathcal{P}$HOTOGRAPH

NEPHEWS AND NIECES

YOUR SPOUSE'S BROTHERS' AND SISTERS' CHILDREN

NAME	CHILD OF/AND	DATE OF BIRTH

Where did you first meet them? How old were they? Did any of them come to your wedding?

What is each of them doing now?

PHOTOGRAPH

GRANDCHILDREN

Your Children's Children

NAME	CHILD OF/AND	DATE OF BIRTH

How old were you when your first grandchild was born? What do you particularly enjoy about being a grandparent?

What is their name for you? Do you find it difficult not to spoil them?

$\mathcal{G}$RANDCHILDREN

$\mathcal{W}$hat are your happiest memories of them when they were young?

....

....

....

....

....

$\mathcal{D}$o they ever come to stay with you? $\mathcal{H}$ave you ever taken them on holiday?

....

....

....

....

....

$\mathcal{P}$HOTOGRAPHS

GRANDCHILDREN

Have you ever visited their schools? Are any of them good at sports? Or music? Or the arts?

....

....

....

....

....

Have they gone on to further education? If so what did they study?

....

....

....

....

....

PHOTOGRAPHS

GRANDCHILDREN

What career did each of them choose? **D**id they move away from home when they started earning?

....
....
....
....
....
....

What do you think has been the most interesting thing that has happened to each of them?

....
....
....
....
....
....

Have any of them married? **I**f so, to whom?

NAME	MARRIED	PLACE	DATE

GREAT-GRANDCHILDREN

YOUR GRANDCHILDREN'S CHILDREN

NAME	CHILD OF/AND	DATE OF BIRTH

How old were you when your first great-grandchild was born? Have you met all your great-grandchildren?

In what ways does the relationship with your great-grandchildren differ from that with your grandchildren?

GREAT-GRANDCHILDREN

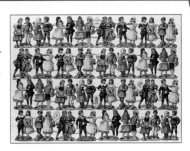

How do you view the world into which your great-grandchildren have been born? What are your hopes for each of them?

....
....
....
....

What features from your own childhood do you think they would benefit from? And what aspects of their childhood would you like to have had as part of yours?

....
....
....

What do you think is the most important single thing for a young person to remember?

....
....
....

Is there anything you would particularly like to do together with your great-grandchildren?

....
....

PHOTOGRAPH

....
....
....

OTHER RELATIONS

'Other relations' might include your own or your childrens' godparents and guardians, your second cousins, children to whom you are yourself a godparent or a guardian, and any step-relations. This page is for your memories of them.

....

....

....

....

....

....

....

....

....

....

....

....

....

*P*HOTOGRAPH

....

....

....

....

....

....

....

....

....

SPECIAL FRIENDS

For notes and memories about the other people who have played an important part in the family's life, but are not related to you by birth or marriage. Old friends from schooldays who became unofficial 'aunts' and 'uncles' to children and grandchildren, people you have come to know well at work or socially . . . in fact anyone who has been important in your life, or particularly valued as a friend, may find a place here.

....

....

....

....

....

....

....

....

....

....

....

....

....

....

....

....

$$\mathscr{P}\text{HOTOGRAPH}$$

GREAT-GREAT-UNCLES AND GREAT-GREAT-AUNTS

GREAT-GRANDPARENTS

YOUR GREAT-GRANDFATHER'S BROTHERS AND SISTERS
Your Great-Great-Uncles and Great-Great-Aunts

YOUR FATHER'S FATHER'S FATHER
Your Great-Grandfather – **page 6**

YOUR GREAT-GRANDMOTHER'S BROTHERS AND SISTERS
Your Great-Great-Uncles and Great-Great-Aunts

YOUR FATHER'S FATHER'S MOTHER
Your Great-Grandmother – **page 6**

YOUR GREAT-GRANDFATHER'S BROTHERS AND SISTERS
Your Great-Great-Uncles and Great-Great-Aunts

YOUR FATHER'S MOTHER'S FATHER
Your Great-Grandfather – **page 7**

YOUR GREAT-GRANDMOTHER'S BROTHERS AND SISTERS
Your Great-Great-Uncles and Great-Great-Aunts

YOUR FATHER'S MOTHER'S MOTHER
Your Great-Grandmother – **page 7**

YOUR GREAT-GRANDFATHER'S BROTHERS AND SISTERS
Your Great-Great-Uncles and Great-Great-Aunts

YOUR MOTHER'S FATHER'S FATHER
Your Great-Grandfather – **page 8**

YOUR GREAT-GRANDMOTHER'S BROTHERS AND SISTERS
Your Great-Great-Uncles and Great-Great-Aunts

YOUR MOTHER'S FATHER'S MOTHER
Your Great-Grandmother – **page 8**

YOUR GREAT-GRANDFATHER'S BROTHERS AND SISTERS
Your Great-Great-Uncles and Great-Great-Aunts

YOUR MOTHER'S MOTHER'S FATHER
Your Great-Grandfather – **page 9**

YOUR GREAT-GRANDMOTHER'S BROTHERS AND SISTERS
Your Great-Great-Uncles and Great-Great-Aunts

YOUR MOTHER'S MOTHER'S MOTHER
Your Great-Grandmother – **page 9**

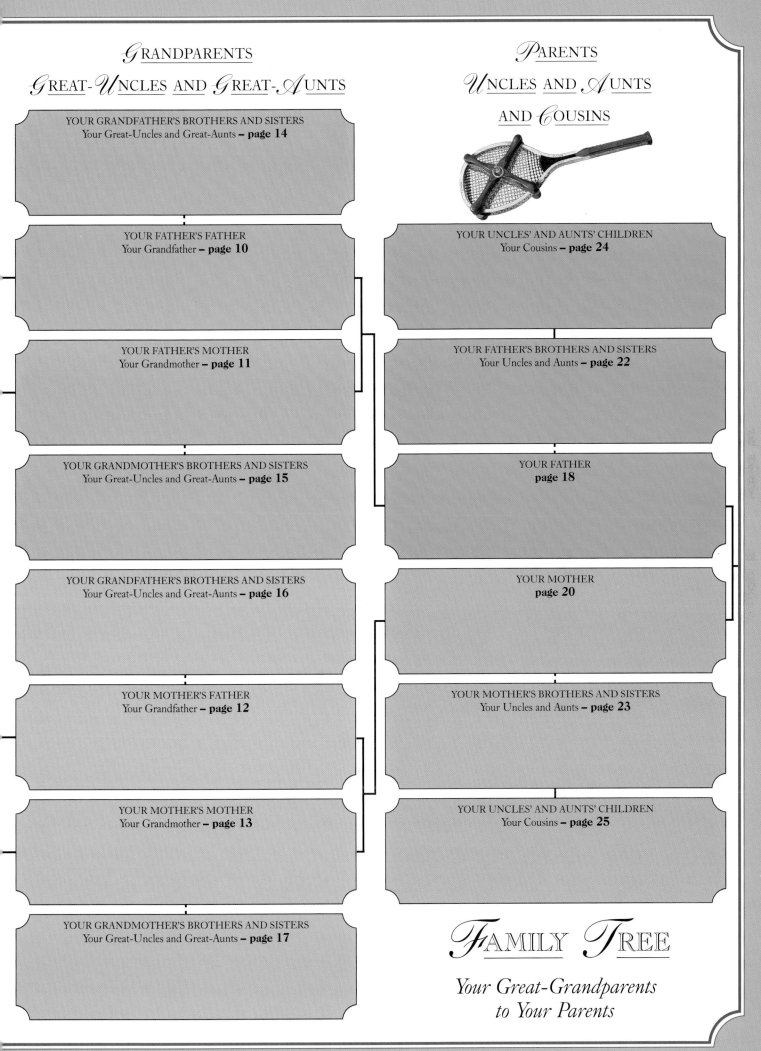

𝓕AMILY 𝓣REE

*Your Great-Grandparents
to Your Parents*

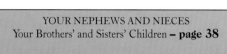

𝒴OURSELF AND 𝒴OUR 𝒮POUSE
ℬROTHERS AND 𝒮ISTERS
𝒩EPHEWS AND 𝒩IECES

𝒮ONS AND 𝒟AUGHTERS

YOUR NEPHEWS AND NIECES
Your Brothers' and Sisters' Children **– page 38**

YOUR BROTHERS AND SISTERS
page 28

YOURSELF
page 26

YOUR SPOUSE
page 30

YOUR SPOUSE'S BROTHERS AND SISTERS
page 34

YOUR SPOUSE'S NEPHEWS AND NIECES
Your Spouse's Brothers' and Sisters' Children **– page 39**

YOUR CHILDREN
page 36

ℱAMILY 𝒯REE

Yourself and Your Spouse
to Your Great-Grandchildren

GRANDCHILDREN

YOUR CHILDREN'S CHILDREN
page 40

GREAT-GRANDCHILDREN

YOUR GRANDCHILDREN'S CHILDREN
page 44

The Family before 1850

What is the earliest mention you have been able to find of your family? **W**ho did you find and where did he or she live?

....
....
....
....
....
....
....
....

Do you know where the family name comes from and whether it has any particular meaning?

....
....
....
....
....
....

❖— Mementoes —❖

What part of the world did your forebears come from, both on your mother's and your father's side?

Were there any prominent people on either side of the family?

·—— Father's ancestors ——·

·—— Mother's ancestors ——·

What were the most important things that happened to the family?

THE NATION
1850 - 1879

1850 Charles Dickens' *David Copperfield* published
1850 England and France joined by submarine cable
1851 The Great Exhibition held at Crystal Palace in Hyde Park
1852 Independence of South African Republic recognised
1853 David Livingstone starts exploring Zambesi River
1854 Outbreak of Crimean War against Russia
1854 Florence Nightingale reforms army's medical and sanitary conditions in Crimea
1854 North Eastern Railway completed
1855 David Livingstone discovers Victoria Falls
1856 Victoria Cross award for gallantry instituted
1856 Treaty of Paris ends Crimean War
1856 Bessemer converts iron into steel
1858 'Big Ben' cast in Whitechapel
1859 Darwin's *Origin of Species* published
1861 Post Office Savings Bank opens
1862 Great Eastern Railway completed
1863 Football Association founded
1863 Wedding of Edward, Prince of Wales, to Princess Alexandra of Denmark
1867 Reform Act extends franchise to working classes in towns
1867 Canada becomes a dominion of the British Empire
1868 Gladstone becomes Prime Minister
1868 Last public execution of a woman
1869 Suez Canal opens
1870 First postcards and ½d. stamps
1870 First Barnardo children's home opens
1871 Rugby Football Union formed
1874 Lawn tennis patented by an Englishman
1876 Queen Victoria declared Empress of India
1876 Telephone invented by Alexander Graham Bell
1877 First dry photographic plates developed
1879 Tay railway bridge collapses, killing 90
1879 First issue of 'Boy's Own Paper'

*** THE FAMILY ***
1850-1879

During this period, Britain's influence around the world was very considerable. Many young men worked or fought overseas for at least a few years. At home, industry continued to grow very fast and the population of the towns and cities increased rapidly. What were your parents' families lives like during these three decades?

MEMENTOES

*** OR ***

PHOTOGRAPHS

Which members of the family were born in this period?

FATHER'S ANCESTORS

MOTHER'S ANCESTORS

Where did they live? How did they earn their living?

The Nation 1880-1899

1880	First telephone directory published
1880	Frozen meat first imported from Australia
1880	First issue of 'Girl's Own Paper'
1881	Postal Orders first issued
1882	First electric tramcars appear in London
1882	Attempted assassination of Queen Victoria
1883	Boys' Brigade founded in Glasgow
1883	Fabian Society founded
1883	Sickness Insurance introduced
1884	Reform Act extends franchise to working classes in rural districts
1885	Motorcycle invented in England
1885	General Gordon killed at Khartoum
1885	First bars of Sunlight soap manufactured by William Lever
1885	Sullivan writes *The Mikado*
1886	'The Times' prints the first personal column in its classified pages
1886	Gladstone introduces Home Rule for Ireland Bill
1887	Queen Victoria's Silver Jubilee
1888	Pneumatic tyre invented by John Dunlop
1888	English Football League formed
1888	W.G. Grace begins 10-year captaincy of England Cricket team
1889	London dock strike
1890	Electrified underground railway opens between City and South London
1890	Construction of the Forth Railway Bridge completed
1891	London-Paris telephone service starts
1891	Construction of Blackpool Tower begun
1892	Independent Labour Party established
1894	Urban and Rural District Councils and Parish Councils established
1895	The National Trust founded by Octavia Hill
1896	Modern Olympic Games revived in Athens
1897	Queen Victoria's Diamond Jubilee
1897	Electron discovered by Sir Joseph Thompson
1899	Boer War starts

The Family 1880-1899

There were many social and economic developments during the last twenty years of the nineteenth century. At the same time, technical and industrial advances continued, particularly in transport and communications. What were the major events in the life of the family during this period?

Photographs
═ or ═
Mementoes

Which members of the family were born during these two decades?

━━━ *Father's side* ━━━

━━━ *Mother's side* ━━━

Which of these people did you or your parents meet? What do you know about them and their lives?

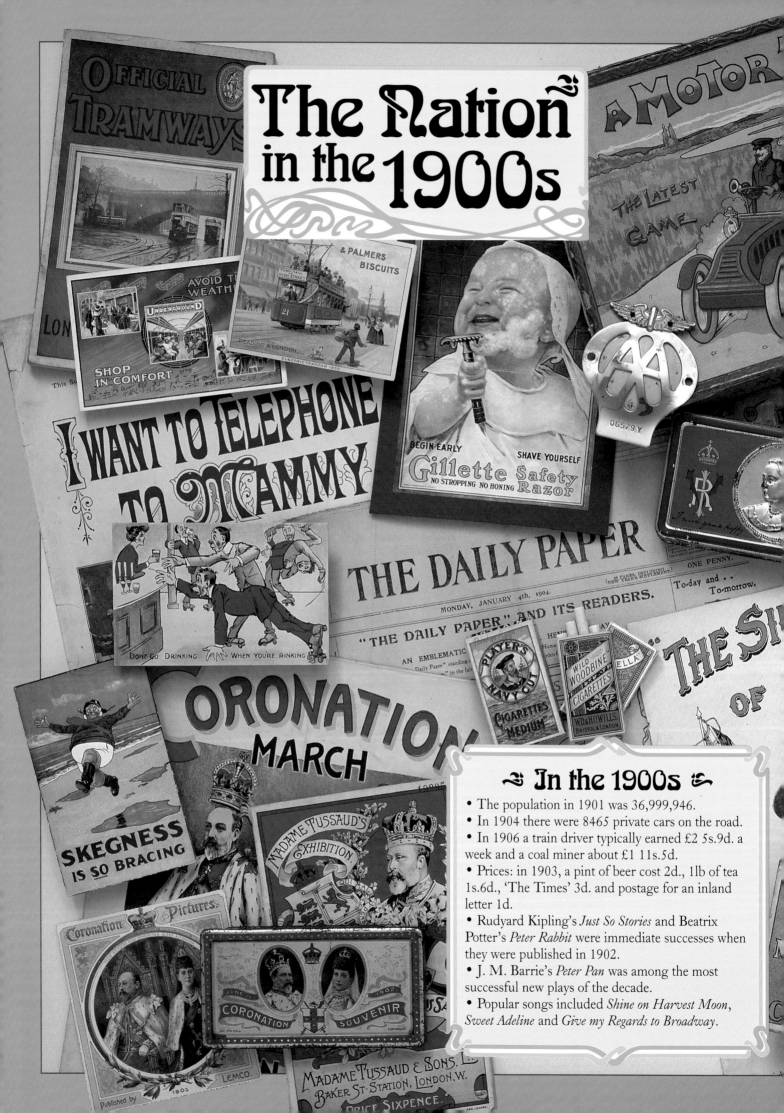

The Nation in the 1900s

In the 1900s

- The population in 1901 was 36,999,946.
- In 1904 there were 8465 private cars on the road.
- In 1906 a train driver typically earned £2 5s.9d. a week and a coal miner about £1 11s.5d.
- Prices: in 1903, a pint of beer cost 2d., 1lb of tea 1s.6d., 'The Times' 3d. and postage for an inland letter 1d.
- Rudyard Kipling's *Just So Stories* and Beatrix Potter's *Peter Rabbit* were immediate successes when they were published in 1902.
- J. M. Barrie's *Peter Pan* was among the most successful new plays of the decade.
- Popular songs included *Shine on Harvest Moon*, *Sweet Adeline* and *Give my Regards to Broadway*.

1900   Coca Cola first sold in the UK
1900   'Daily Express' first published
1900   British Labour Party founded
1900   Siege of Mafeking relieved by British forces under Baden-Powell
1901   Commonwealth of Australia formed
1901   King Camp Gillette patents safety razor
1901   Queen Victoria dies, aged 81
1901   The London United Tramways launch first electric trams
1901   Brownie camera No. 2 goes on sale
1902   Underground Electric Railway Company formed
1902   Empire Day first celebrated
1902   Boer War ends in British victory
1902   Coronation of King Edward VII
1902   First conviction made in Britain on evidence of fingerprints
1903   First radio message transmitted from England to USA
1903   'Daily Mirror' first published
1903   First motor taxis appear in London
1904   Electric mainline train service opens
1904   Registration plates first used on motor cars
1904   Books of postage stamps issued
1905   Automobile Association formed
1905   Footballers' maximum wage set at £4 per week
1905   Sinn Fein founded by Arthur Griffith
1906   Trade Disputes Act legalises peaceful picketing
1907   Brooklands motor racing track opens
1907   Boy-Scout movement founded by Baden-Powell
1908   England win first-ever international football match, against Austria
1908   Old-age pension of 5s.0d. a week granted to single people over 70
1908   Olympic Games held in London
1909   Victoria and Albert Museum opens in Kensington, London
1909   Louis Bleriot flies his monoplane across English Channel
1909   First Woolworth's store opens, in Liverpool

The Family in the 1900s

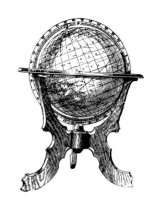

$\mathcal{D}$id any of your relations serve in the Boer War? $\mathcal{O}$r overseas in the Empire?

Important Family Events

NAME	DATE	EVENT

Photographs
~ or ~
Mementoes

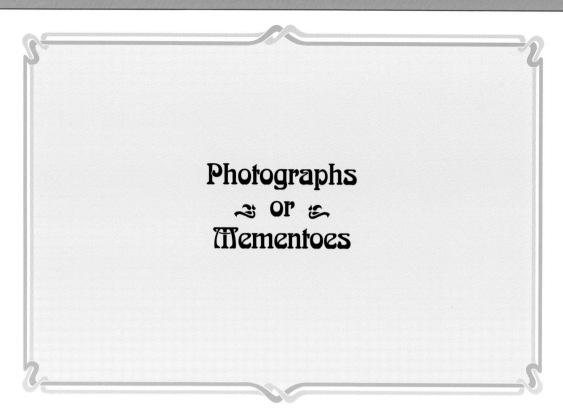

Did any of them speak about the death of Queen Victoria or the coronation of King Edward VII?

Did any of them tell you of the first time they saw an aeroplane or a motor car? **D**o you have any mementoes

from that time?

The Nation in the 1910s

WELDON'S LADIES'
MAY 1918
No. 457.

The New Game
BRITISH v GERMANS
THE GREAT WAR.
BRITISH MANUFACTURE

Patriotic Autograph Christmas Stationery
Box Number 512.

MAN. EMPLOYED CONTRIBUTOR
NATIONAL HEALTH INSURANCE. INSURANCE BOOK.

MINISTRY OF FOOD.
NATIONAL RATION BOOK (B).
INSTRUCTIONS.
COSFORD, R.D. Date Oct

JOHN BULL WAR

THE COMPACT
ACTIVE SERVICE
KHAKI KOMBINATION KANDLEBOX
REG? No 658484.

BANK IN THE TANK TANK TANK
BANK BANK BANK

PEACE

I WAS NEARLY SQUEEZED TO DEATH IN THE CROWD!

1914-1919 PEACE
LIBERTY JUSTICE TRUTH HONOUR

THE WRECK OF THE TITANIC
Descriptive Musical Sketch For the PIANO

∼∼ In the 1910s ∼∼

• The 1911 census showed a population of 40,831,396.
• In 1914 there were 132,015 private cars.
• In 1913 the monthly salary for a teacher was about £15 0s.0d. and the weekly wage for a train driver was £2 0s.6d.
• Prices: by 1915, the price of a pint of beer had risen to 3d., 1lb of tea to 2s.0d. 'The Times' was still 3d. and inland letter postage 1d.
• The *Birth of a Nation* was the biggest-earning film and Bernard Shaw's new play *Pygmalion* was a West End success.
• *Alexander's Ragtime Band* and *Chinatown, My Chinatown* were two of the most popular songs.

1910	King Edward VII dies
1910	Dr Crippen hanged in London for poisoning his wife
1910	First Labour Exchanges open
1911	First trolley-buses appear
1911	MP's annual salary fixed at £400
1911	Coronation of King George V
1911	Suffragettes riot in Whitehall
1911	First National Health Bill introduced
1912	Captain Scott dies on way back from South Pole
1912	'Titanic' sinks after hitting an iceberg, with loss of 1513 lives
1912	National Insurance introduced
1913	Sickness, unemployment and maternity benefits introduced
1913	Charlie Chaplin makes his first film
1914	Britain declares war on Germany
1914	Panama Canal opens
1914	Builders', miners' and railway workers' strike
1914	Single bomb dropped on Dover – Britain's first air-raid
1915	Photos first required in British passports
1915	Germany uses poison gas for first time, at Ypres
1915	Passenger liner 'Lusitania' torpedoed by Germans, with loss of 1198 lives
1915	First air-raid on London
1915	The Women's Institute founded
1915	Edith Cavell shot by German firing squad
1916	Military conscription begins
1916	Easter rebellion in Dublin against British rule
1916	Military tanks first used in the British army
1916	First Battle of the Somme results in 420,000 casualties
1917	United States declares war on Germany
1918	Women first permitted to vote in Britain
1918	Royal Air Force formed
1918	First World War ends
1919	First British airline opens with two-seater single-engine biplane
1919	First meeting of League of Nations in Paris

The Family in the 1910s

Which members of the family served in the First World War? What descriptions did they give of life during those years?

....

....

....

....

....

....

....

....

....

....

....

~~~ Photographs ~~~

....

....

....

....

∼∼ Important Family Events ∼∼

NAME	DATE	EVENT

At home, in what way did life change because of the war? And what was it like immediately after the war ended?

Can any of your relations remember hearing about the sinking of the 'Titanic', or the coronation of King George V?

Did any of them join the newly-formed Women's Institute?

THE NATION IN THE 1920s

I'M LITTLE MISS NOBODY AT WORK—

Doing the FOX TROT.

You have to wash your Neck when you've got your hair Bobbed.

The SCHNEIDER TROPHY CONTEST 1929
Sept. 6th & 7th

BANK HOLIDAY WHERE TO GO

BY TRAIN, TRAM AND MOTOR BUS AUGUST 1926

Meltis LITTLE PRINCESS Assorted Chocolates

Meltis LTD. BEDFORD & LONDON, ENGLAND.

HALF POUND (INCLUDING FOILS)

Miss 1927

"FELIX KEPT UN

Royal Enfield

THE FAMOUS 6 H.P. ROYAL ENFIEL

1928-9 HORNBY BOOK OF TRAINS

6100

PRICE THREEPENCE.

"SAVE BEFORE YOU SPEND": BY G. WARD

SUNDAY · PICTORIAL

OF ANY OTHER PICTURE PAPER IN THE WORLD

SUNDAY, NOVEMBER 24, 1929 Twopence

WEATHER STOPS R10

R 100

◤◤ IN THE 1920s ◢◢

- In 1921 the population of Great Britain was 42,769,196.
- By 1924 the number of private cars had increased to 482,356.
- In 1920, a GP earned on average £756 a year and a farm worker £1 17s.10d. a week.
- In 1923 you would have paid 10d. for 8 Players No.3 cigarettes and £175 for a 2-seater Morris Cowley. In 1927 a radio licence cost 10s.0d.
- The most popular names for babies born in 1925 were Joan and John.
- 1920s hits included: the play *The Ghost Train*; the film *The Jazz Singer* (the first full-length talkie); the song *Avalon*; the fox-trot and the bobbed hairstyle.

1920	Oxford University awards degrees to women
1920	First Hornby train sets produced
1921	Gordon Richards has first of 4870 wins
1921	British Legion holds its first Poppy Day
1921	Irish Free State established
1922	Tomb of King Tutankhamun discovered
1922	British Broadcasting Company established by group of wireless manufacturers
1922	'Austin Seven', the first British car for the popular market, introduced
1923	Wedding of George, Duke of York, and Lady Elizabeth Bowes-Lyon
1923	First English FA Cup final held at Wembley
1923	£50 million spent by government on unemployment relief
1923	First issue of 'Radio Times'
1923	Chimes of Big Ben first broadcast
1924	Empire Exhibition held at Wembley Stadium
1924	First Labour Government voted to power
1924	USSR recognised by British government
1926	John Logie Baird gives first public demonstration of television
1926	Princess Elizabeth born
1926	3,000,000 join in General Strike
1926	First British Motor Racing Grand Prix, held at Brooklands
1927	Transatlantic telephone service between London and New York opens
1927	First broadcast of a Football League game
1927	Automatic traffic lights come into operation
1927	First London to Brighton veteran car rally
1927	Last Model T Ford produced
1928	Alexander Fleming discovers penicillin
1929	Wall Street stock exchange 'crashes'
1929	Britain wins Schneider Trophy for seaplanes at Southampton
1929	Trial flight of airship R100

THE FAMILY IN THE 1920s

What effect did the aftermath of the First World War have on the family? Was it a decade of great changes for them?

....

....

....

....

....

....

....

....

....

IMPORTANT FAMILY EVENTS

NAME	DATE	EVENT

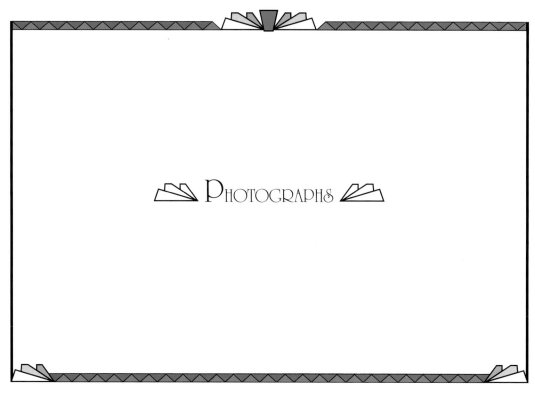

PHOTOGRAPHS

This period also has the reputation of being a time of celebration. Can anyone in the family remember (or remember being told about) the happier side of life in the twenties – cars, dancing, motion pictures?

Did anyone go to the Empire Exhibition, or the first FA Cup Final? Have you any souvenirs from the period?

THE NATION IN THE 1930s

═ IN THE 1930s ═

- In 1931, 44,795,357 people lived in Britain.
- By 1934 there were 1,333,590 private cars.
- Typical weekly pay-packets in 1935: clerical worker £3 13s.10d.; coal miner £2 4s.8d.
- In 1932 a bottle of Gordon's Gin cost 12s.6d., 10 Players Navy Cut Cigarettes cost 6d and a Mars Bar 2d. By 1935 a pint of beer cost 7d., 1lb of tea 1s.4d., 'The Times' 4d. and inland letter postage was 1½d.
- At the cinema: *The Wizard of Oz*, *Gone with the Wind*, the Marx Brothers' *A Night at the Opera* and Walt Disney's *Snow White*.
- People were singing *On the Sunny Side of the Street*, playing Monopoly and Bezique and going to see Noel Coward's *Private Lives*.

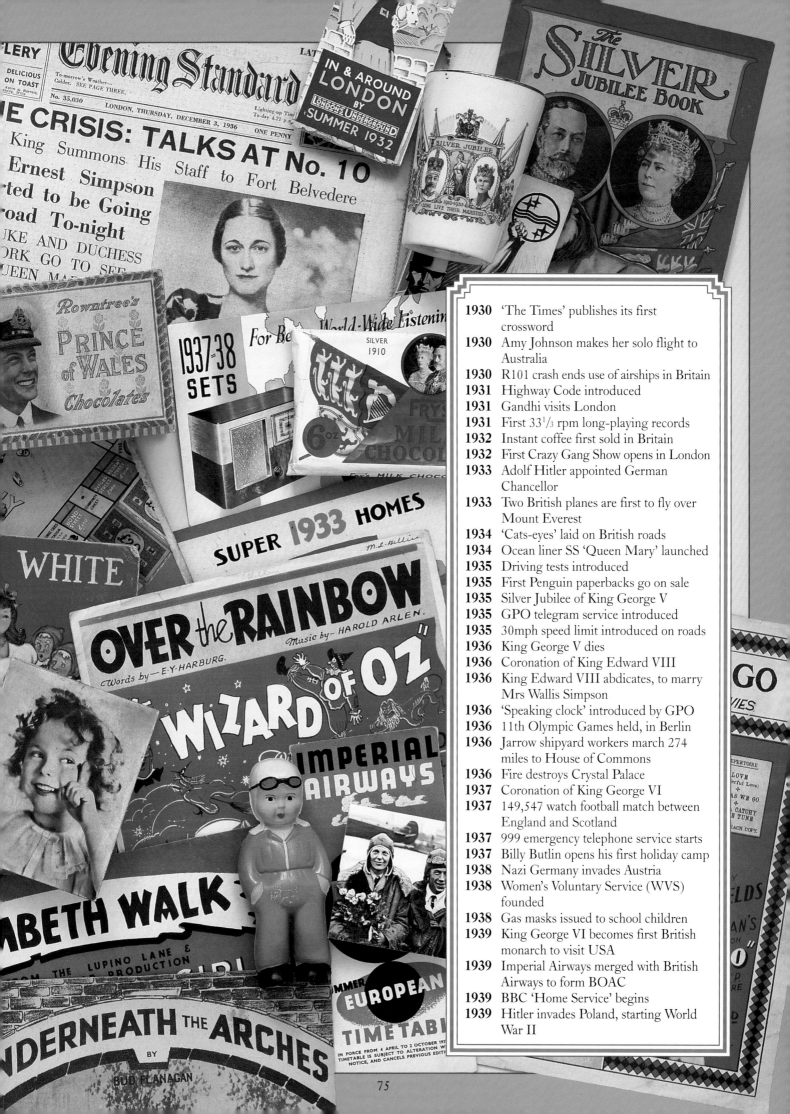

1930	'The Times' publishes its first crossword
1930	Amy Johnson makes her solo flight to Australia
1930	R101 crash ends use of airships in Britain
1931	Highway Code introduced
1931	Gandhi visits London
1931	First 33⅓ rpm long-playing records
1932	Instant coffee first sold in Britain
1932	First Crazy Gang Show opens in London
1933	Adolf Hitler appointed German Chancellor
1933	Two British planes are first to fly over Mount Everest
1934	'Cats-eyes' laid on British roads
1934	Ocean liner SS 'Queen Mary' launched
1935	Driving tests introduced
1935	First Penguin paperbacks go on sale
1935	Silver Jubilee of King George V
1935	GPO telegram service introduced
1935	30mph speed limit introduced on roads
1936	King George V dies
1936	Coronation of King Edward VIII
1936	King Edward VIII abdicates, to marry Mrs Wallis Simpson
1936	'Speaking clock' introduced by GPO
1936	11th Olympic Games held, in Berlin
1936	Jarrow shipyard workers march 274 miles to House of Commons
1936	Fire destroys Crystal Palace
1937	Coronation of King George VI
1937	149,547 watch football match between England and Scotland
1937	999 emergency telephone service starts
1937	Billy Butlin opens his first holiday camp
1938	Nazi Germany invades Austria
1938	Women's Voluntary Service (WVS) founded
1938	Gas masks issued to school children
1939	King George VI becomes first British monarch to visit USA
1939	Imperial Airways merged with British Airways to form BOAC
1939	BBC 'Home Service' begins
1939	Hitler invades Poland, starting World War II

THE FAMILY
IN THE 1930s

This was a decade of financial difficulty for many. How did events during these years affect the family? Was anyone out of work during the Depression?

= PHOTOGRAPHS =

≡ IMPORTANT FAMILY EVENTS ≡

NAME	DATE	EVENT

Can anyone remember the fire at Crystal Palace? Had anyone travelled by 'plane by the end of the thirties?

Did anyone hear the broadcast declaring that Britain was at war with Germany? What were the immediate effects of this announcement?

THE NATION IN THE 1940s

IN THE 1940s

- There was no 1941 census, but before war broke out the population was 46,466,689.
- By 1944 the number of private cars in Britain had fallen to 773,034.
- In 1948 65% of men and 41% of women smoked.
- In 1947, a train driver's weekly wage was £6 6s.6d. and a bricklayer's £5 15s.6d.
- Ration allowances per person per week in 1940 were: 8oz sugar, 2oz tea, 4oz butter and 2s.2d. worth of meat.
- The films: *Bambi, Citizen Kane, Casablanca*. The play: *An Inspector Calls*. The book: George Orwell's *Animal Farm*.
- Most toys were home-made because of the war.

1940	Sir Winston Churchill becomes Prime Minister of Coalition government
1940	Food rationing starts
1940	Home Guard formed
1940	Evacuation of British forces from Dunkirk
1940	Battle of Britain
1941	Nylon first produced in Britain, at Coventry
1941	'Bismarck' sunk by three British battleships
1941	Britain and US declare war on Japan
1942	Soap rationing begins
1943	The Mohne, Eider and Sorpe dams in Germany breached
1944	Allied Army landings in Italy begin
1944	Pay As You Earn income tax introduced
1944	Allied landings off coast of Normandy
1944	First flying bomb falls on England
1944	British airborne invasions of Arnhem and Eindhoven
1945	Yalta conference in Crimea results in founding of United Nations
1945	Hitler commits suicide
1945	War in Europe officially ends
1945	Family Allowance payment of 5s.0d. per week introduced
1945	Atomic bomb dropped on Hiroshima
1945	Japanese surrender ends World War II
1945	Bread rationing begins
1945	Bank of England nationalised
1947	Coal industry nationalised
1947	First supersonic flight
1947	Worst floods ever recorded in England
1947	School-leaving age raised to 15
1947	Princess Elizabeth marries Prince Philip
1948	Railways nationalised
1948	First full-size supermarket opens
1948	National Health Service established
1948	Bread rationing ends
1948	First Morris Minor car appears
1948	London hosts Olympic Games
1949	Clothes rationing ends
1949	First comprehensive school opens
1949	North Atlantic Treaty Organisation (NATO) created

THE FAMILY IN THE 1940s

How did the Second World War change the family's life? Who fought in the War? Were there any casualties?

....

....

....

....

....

....

....

....

....

....

....

....

....

....

....

....

....

....

....

■ PHOTOGRAPHS ■

══ IMPORTANT FAMILY EVENTS ══

NAME	DATE	EVENT

What was it like for those left behind? Were any of the young ones evacuated? Where did they go? How did those left at home cope with war-time life?

What was it like when the war ended? What was the spirit of the country at that time? How soon did life begin to return to normal?

THE NATION IN THE 1950s

LIVE IT UP!

FESTIVAL OF BRITAIN 1951

Made by Kodak 'BROWNIE' 127 camera

24/6 INC. TAX

BILL HALEY AND HIS COMETS

EXTENDED PLAY RECORD

Nº 18

EXCITING GLAMOUR PHOTOS

Marilyn MONROE

The new Sensational Dansette

Kodak Brownie 127 CAMERA

Welcome to LONDON

LONDON TRANSPORT
BRITISH RAILWAYS

Picture Show
THE PAPER FOR PEOPLE WHO GO TO THE PICTURES
& FILM

FINAL NIGHT EXTRA

Evening Standard
FRIDAY, FEBRUARY 8, 1952 • Three-halfpence

On the roofs, on the balconies, in the people crowd to hear the Pro

GOD SAVE THE QUEEN

O! for OLIVER TYPEWRITER

Elizabeth R CORONATION TUESDAY 2 JUNE 1953

LONDON TRANSPORT
BRITISH RAILWAYS

🌹 IN THE 1950s 🌹

- The 1951 census totalled 48,854,303.
- By 1954 there were 3,172,869 cars in Britain.
- In 1953, 59% of men and 36% of women smoked.
- Wages rose rapidly: in 1955 a clerical worker could expect to earn £10 1s.0d. a week, a coal miner £8 6s.0d., and a solicitor £2086 a year.
- Prices rose too: by 1955 a pint of beer had gone up to 1s.3$\frac{1}{4}$d., 1lb of tea to 4s.6d. and inland letter post to 2$\frac{1}{2}$d. A Kodak Brownie Box camera cost £1 19s.9d., a 'Noddy' soft toy £1, and a Dansette Radiogram £31 10s.0d.
- Top children's names in 1950: Susan and David.
- Films of the 50s: *The Ten Commandments*, *High Society* and *East of Eden*.

1950	Election returns televised in Britain for first time
1950	Petrol and soap rationing ends
1950	India becomes a democratic Republic
1950	Coronation Stone stolen from Westminster Abbey
1950	Marcus Morris, a clergyman, founds 'Eagle' comic
1951	First Miss World contest
1951	Festival of Britain, to mark centenary of the Great Exhibition
1951	First zebra crossings
1952	Death of King George VI
1952	Identity cards abolished in Britain
1952	Last London tram runs
1952	BBC radio broadcasts first 'Goon Show'
1953	Sugar and sweet rationing ends
1953	Edmund Hillary and Sherpa Tensing climb Everest
1953	Coronation of HM Queen Elizabeth II
1954	Roger Bannister runs a mile in under four minutes
1954	Bill Haley's 'Rock Around the Clock' recorded – the best-selling pop record of all time
1954	All food rationing ends
1955	First commercial appears on television
1956	First yellow 'no parking' lines
1956	Premium Bonds go on sale
1956	First Eurovision song contest
1957	The Queen makes her first Christmas television broadcast
1958	Prince Charles created Prince of Wales
1958	Eight Manchester United players die in aircraft crash
1958	9000 join first CND protest march from London to Aldermaston
1958	Parking meters come into operation
1958	Debutantes presented at Court for the last time
1958	First women peers in the House of Lords
1958	Work starts on Forth Road Bridge
1959	First section of the M1 motorway opened
1959	Postcodes added to all addresses

THE FAMILY
IN THE 1950s

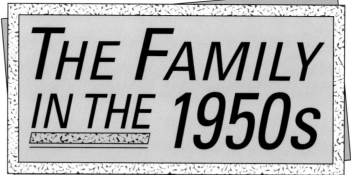

*M*any remember this as a decade of optimism and rising standards of living. *W*hat events do the family recall?

☆☆ IMPORTANT FAMILY EVENTS ☆☆

NAME	DATE	EVENT

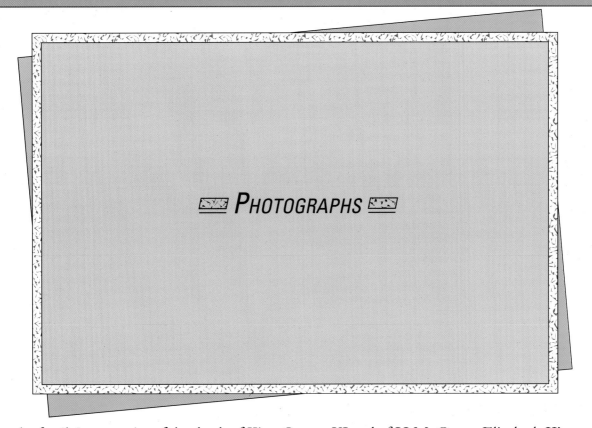

⬛ *P*HOTOGRAPHS ⬛

*W*hat are the family's memories of the death of King George VI and of H.M. Queen Elizabeth II's coronation?

*T*his was the decade in which commercial television started, the first motorway was built, the last London tram ran and package holidays started. *H*ow did all this affect the family?

The Nation in the 1960s

PARLOPHONE

SAW HER STANDING THERE
MISERY • ANNA • CHAINS

mono

No. 1

Twist and Shout • The Beatles

mono

Twist and Shout
THE BEATLES

DINKY TOYS

THUNDERBALL

RADIO CAROLINE
THE ALL DAY MUSIC STATION

Featuring the TOP DEE JAYS and new personal stories of the STARS

WILLIE
by Syd Green

WORLD CUP WILLIE

WORLD

NEWS OF THE WORLD

EMPIRE NEWS No. 6,239. PRICE SIXPENCE

SUNDAY, JUNE 9, 1963

Confessions of Christine

BY SPEAR

PRODUCTION

CORONATION STREET

Queen Elizabeth 2

CUNARD

WATNEY MANN WORLD CUP ALE

SPECIAL PALE ALE

JULES RIMET CUP
WORLD CHAMPIONSHIP
ENGLAND 1966 JULY 11-30
EVERTON·SHEFFIELD·SUNDERLAND·ASTON VILLA· MANCHESTER · MIDDLESBROUGH· WHITE CITY

✿✿ IN THE 1960s ✿✿

- In 1961 the UK population was 51,283,892.
- By 1964 there were 8,436,193 private cars, a police constable's weekly wage was £13 9s.6d. and a bricklayer's £17 3s.0d. 54% of men and 41% of women smoked.
- By '65 a pint of beer cost 1s.9d., 1lb of tea 8s.0d., 'The Times' 6d. and an inland letter 3d. A gallon of petrol cost 5s.2d. and a Mini Cooper £679.
- The most popular name for a girl born in 1965 was Tracey.
- Hits of the 60s: TV: *Coronation Street* and *Thunderbirds*. Pop Music: The Beatles. Toys: Sindy and Action Man. Fashion: Mary Quant. Films: *The Sound of Music*, *The Seven Year Itch* and *Mary Poppins*. Plays: *West Side Story* and *The Caretaker*.

DAVID TOFF MUSIC PUBLISHING CO. LTD. LO

VENIR PROGRAMME

1960 MOT tests on motor vehicles introduced
1960 Hovercraft enters commercial service
1960 First traffic wardens appear in London
1960 Britain's first nuclear-powered submarine launched
1961 *New English Bible* published
1961 Cash betting at betting shops made legal
1962 Trolleybuses run for the last time in London
1962 First James Bond film, 'Dr No', released
1963 £2,631,684 stolen from Post Office train in the Great Train Robbery
1963 President Kennedy assassinated in Dallas
1963 Christine Keeler jailed in Profumo Affair trial
1963 'From Me to You' becomes the first of four successive number one hits for The Beatles
1964 Harold Wilson becomes Prime Minister
1964 Sir Winston Churchill makes his last appearance in the House of Commons
1964 Radio Caroline starts transmission
1965 Sir Winston Churchill dies, aged 90
1965 Cigarette advertisements banned on TV
1965 70mph speed limit introduced
1966 Seaman's strike, the longest in Britain since World War II
1966 England hosts and wins the football World Cup
1966 Severn Bridge opens
1967 First North Sea gas pumped ashore
1967 Oil tanker 'Torrey Canyon' wrecked on the Pollard Rock
1967 Francis Chichester sails round the world solo
1967 British liner 'QE2' launched
1967 BBC Radio 1 goes on air
1968 Abortion legalised
1969 Investiture of Prince of Wales at Caernarfon Castle
1969 Neil Armstrong sets foot on the moon
1969 First colour television programmes broadcast
1969 Abolition of the death penalty for murder

The Family in the 1960s

Who remembers England winning the Football World Cup? **O**r seeing pictures of Neil Armstrong walking on the moon?

❀❀ Photographs ❀❀

❀❀ Important Family Events ❀❀

NAME	DATE	EVENT

Does anyone remember where they were and what they were doing when they heard that President Kennedy had been killed?

What are other memories of this decade, the Swinging Sixties?

Your guide to decimal currency in the Post Office.

Cadbury's Fruit & Nut

1/- 5p

BOURNVILLE CHOCOLATE

DECIMAL dp COINAGE CONVERTER

3p

THE DECIMAL COINAGE

The Nation in the 1970s

All change!

Mail

MOUNTBATTEN SPECIAL ISSUE

DECIMAL DAY
MONDAY 15th FEBRUARY 1971

The Silver Jubilee Project Book

MURDER OF LORD LOUIS

Mountbatten

1952 THE QUEENS SILVER JUBILEE 1977

STAR TREK

NCC-1701

ENTERPRISE & SPACE LAB

The World's First Reusable Orbital System!

✪ In the 1970s ✪

- By 1971 the population was 53,978,538.
- In 1974 there were 13,947,934 cars in Britain.
- From '70 to '75 a coal miner's weekly wage increased from £16 0s.0d. to £127.70, and a farm worker's from £13 3s.0d. to £66.90.
- Prices also rose: between '71 and '79 the cost of a pint of beer rose from 12p to 34p, 1lb tea from 28p to 35p, 'The Times' from 5p to 15p and inland postage from 3p to 10p. A Mars Bar rose from 4p to 13p.
- Film successes: *Star Wars*, *The Sting* and *The Godfather*. TV favourites: *Starsky & Hutch* and *Star Trek*. Pop Groups: The Osmonds and The Bay City Rollers. Crazes: Skateboards, hot pants, personal calculators, Smurfs and Playpeople.

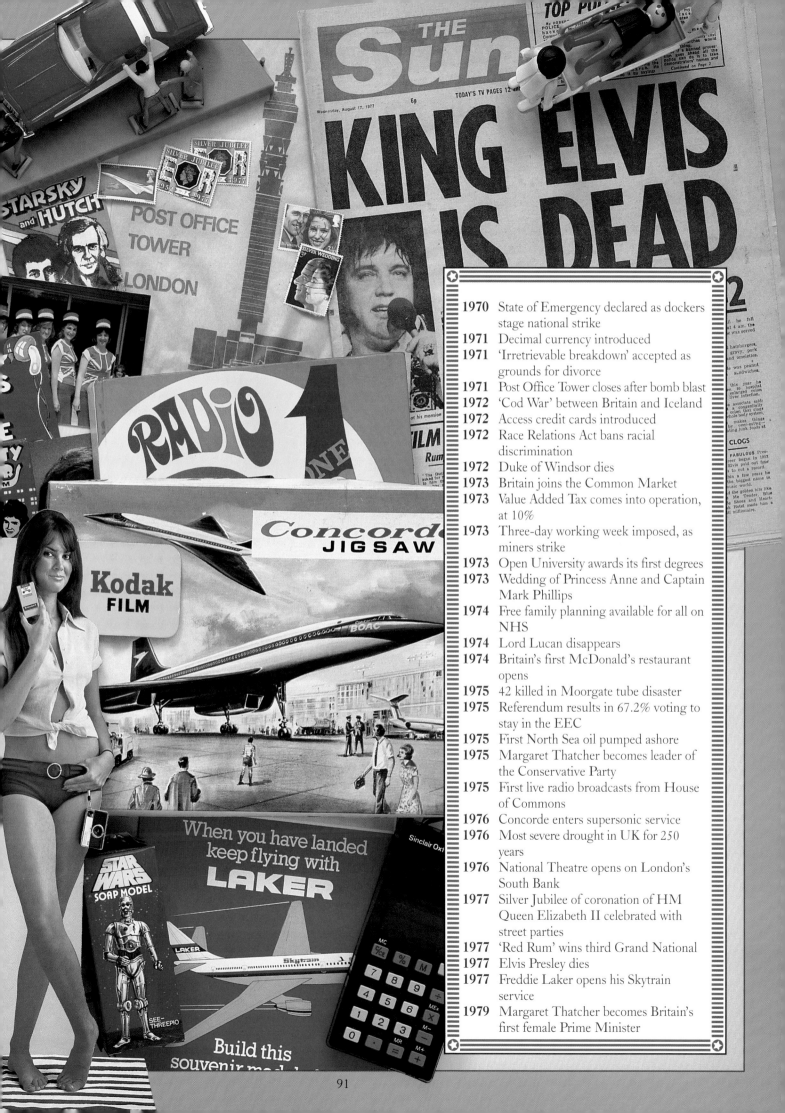

1970 State of Emergency declared as dockers stage national strike
1971 Decimal currency introduced
1971 'Irretrievable breakdown' accepted as grounds for divorce
1971 Post Office Tower closes after bomb blast
1972 'Cod War' between Britain and Iceland
1972 Access credit cards introduced
1972 Race Relations Act bans racial discrimination
1972 Duke of Windsor dies
1973 Britain joins the Common Market
1973 Value Added Tax comes into operation, at 10%
1973 Three-day working week imposed, as miners strike
1973 Open University awards its first degrees
1973 Wedding of Princess Anne and Captain Mark Phillips
1974 Free family planning available for all on NHS
1974 Lord Lucan disappears
1974 Britain's first McDonald's restaurant opens
1975 42 killed in Moorgate tube disaster
1975 Referendum results in 67.2% voting to stay in the EEC
1975 First North Sea oil pumped ashore
1975 Margaret Thatcher becomes leader of the Conservative Party
1975 First live radio broadcasts from House of Commons
1976 Concorde enters supersonic service
1976 Most severe drought in UK for 250 years
1976 National Theatre opens on London's South Bank
1977 Silver Jubilee of coronation of HM Queen Elizabeth II celebrated with street parties
1977 'Red Rum' wins third Grand National
1977 Elvis Presley dies
1977 Freddie Laker opens his Skytrain service
1979 Margaret Thatcher becomes Britain's first female Prime Minister

The Family in the 1970s

A period of social unrest and change – the miners' strike, the three-day week, the Vietnam War. **W**hat was it like for the family?

✪ Important Family Events ✪

NAME	DATE	EVENT

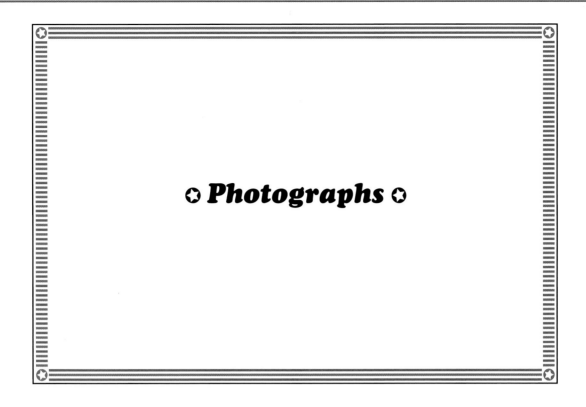

❂ Photographs ❂

What memories are there of decimalisation and of Britain joining the EEC?

....

....

....

....

....

....

....

What were the happiest things that happened to the family in the 70s? **D**oes anyone remember street parties for the Queen's Silver Jubilee?

....

....

....

....

....

....

The Nation in the 1980s

TODAY
TUESDAY MARCH 4, 1986. 18 PENCE

THE TIMES

The Toxteth riot: call for troops on standby

Missiles fly as looters resume battle with Liverpool police

From Nicholas Timmins, Craig Seton and Arthur Osman, Liverpool

THE MARRIAGE OF
The Prince Andrew
with Miss Sarah Ferguson
· 23rd JULY 1986 ·

FAIR PLAY **BINGO**
★★★★★
CAN WIN
NDS WITH
Watch your favourite
newspapers for the
starting date

THE Mirror
PLUS THE
★ WIN A
★ £ MILLIO
★ GAME
SUNDAY Mirror
THIS CARD IS VALUABLE

THE FALKLANDS WAR
A Visual Diary

SONY
STEREO **WALKMAN**

JULY 1981
50p

Carring at Mo

Mrs Thatcher and Mr Gorbachev yesterday

Maggie's nuclear sparring match

CHRIS BUCK
olitical Edito

SOLD FOR £24,750,000
(Yours here for only 20p)

Topps **SPITTING IMAGE**
PICTURE CARDS & BUBBLE GUM

In the 1980s

- In 1981 the population was 54,147,300.
- There were 18,531,744 private cars in 1984 and 34% of the population smoked.
- Between '80 and '89 prices rose: the average house from £27,244 to £74,976; a Mars Bar from 14p to 20p; a pint of beer from 40p to 87p; 1lb tea from 88p to £1.24 and a stamp from 12p to 20p.
- The most popular names for babies born in 1981 were Sarah and Andrew.
- Film of the 80s: *E.T.* Pop stars of the 80s: Michael Jackson, Madonna, Dire Straits, UB40 and The Police. Fads of the 80s: Psion Organisers, Punk, Spitting Image, Trivial Pursuit and Filofaxes.

Year	Event
1980	SAS storms Iranian Embassy and releases hostages
1980	John Lennon shot dead
1980	Bjorn Borg wins Wimbledon for 5th time
1981	First London Marathon
1981	Prince Charles marries Lady Diana Spencer
1981	SDP launched by Labour defectors
1981	First reports of AIDS
1981	Worst riots of century, at Toxteth, Liverpool
1982	Falklands War against Argentina
1982	Pope John Paul II visits Britain
1982	Channel 4 begins broadcasting
1983	Wearing seat-belts in cars made compulsory
1983	One pound coins introduced
1983	Jane Torville and Christopher Dean win third consecutive World Ice Dance title
1983	Conservatives win General Election
1984	Miners' strike
1984	Inaugural flight of Virgin Atlantic
1984	Robert Maxwell buys 'The Mirror'
1985	'Live Aid' pop concert raises more than £50 million for famine relief in Africa
1985	GLC abolished
1985	Start of BBC's 'EastEnders'
1986	Channel Tunnel agreement signed
1986	Corporal punishment abolished in schools
1986	'Today', Britain's first colour newspaper, published
1986	Wedding of Prince Andrew and Sarah Ferguson
1987	Terry Waite disappears in Beirut
1987	'Herald of Free Enterprise' capsizes in Zeebrugge, with loss of 193 lives
1987	'Sunflowers' by Vincent van Gogh sold for £24,750,000
1987	Hurricane force winds kill 19
1987	Margaret Thatcher wins her third General Election
1988	GCSEs replace 'O' levels
1989	Overcrowding at Hillsborough Football Stadium kills 95

The Family in the 1980s

Much came to be taken for granted in the 80s: colour televisions, washing machines, foreign holidays, a generally rising standard of living for most people. **W**hat were your impressions of it all?

Photographs

96

Important Family Events

NAME	DATE	EVENT

Dramatic international events included the Falklands War, the Iranian Embassy siege and hostages being taken in Beirut. What was going on in the family's life?

Does anyone remember the early years of the London Marathon, or celebrating the wedding of Prince Charles and Lady Diana, or seeing Pope John Paul when he visited Britain?

the nation in the 1990s

◀◀ in the 1990s ▶▶

- In 1991 the population was 54,156,067.
- By 1994 there were 23,831,906 cars and only 27% of the population smoked.
- Basic prices in 1993: a pint of beer cost £1.19, 250gm tea 74p, 'The Times' 30p, and a 1st class stamp 25p, the same as a Mars Bar.
- Pop groups: Oasis, Blur and The Spice Girls.
- Films: *Jurrassic Park*, *Reservoir Dogs*, *Toy Story* and *101 Dalmatians*. On stage: *Riverdance* (and *Phantom/Cats/Miss Saigon* etc.). Flops: *Eldorado*. Innovations: alcoholic 'soft' drinks, Wallace & Gromitt, mobile phones, laptop computers, personal CD players, disposable cameras. Toys: Teenage Mutant Hero Turtles, Pogs, Sony PlayStations.

Year	Event
1990	John Major succeeds Margaret Thatcher as Prime Minister
1990	300,000 in riots against Poll Tax
1990	46 die in gales across England
1991	John McCarthy and Terry Waite released
1992	Operation 'Desert Storm' frees Kuwait in Gulf War
1992	Nigel Mansell wins Formula One world championship
1992	Fire destroys part of Windsor Castle
1992	Betty Boothroyd becomes first woman Speaker of House of Commons
1992	UK leaves European Monetary System
1993	Buckingham Palace opens to tourists
1993	Anti-terrorist cordon drawn around the City of London
1994	Inauguration of Channel Tunnel
1994	Church of England ordains women as priests
1994	Shops allowed to open on Sundays
1994	IRA announces total ceasefire
1994	£7 million spent on first day of National Lottery ticket sales
1995	Barings bank collapses, losing £650m
1995	England wins Five-Nations Rugby Cup
1995	First 'Eurostar' trains run through Channel Tunnel
1996	Docklands bomb ends IRA ceasefire
1996	BSE scare causes ban on British beef in Europe (and McDonalds)
1996	Duke and Duchess of York divorce
1996	Prince Charles and Princess Diana divorce
1996	16 children killed by gunman at Dunblane school
1996	Damon Hill wins Formula One world championship
1996	Nelson Mandela visits UK as South African President
1996	Britain hosts 'Euro 96' football championships
1997	66% vote for monarchy in largest TV poll
1997	Tony Blair becomes Prime Minister in Labour landslide
1998	
1999	

the family in the 1990s

W̲hat are your happiest memories of family life in the 1990s?

◀ ◀ i̲m̲p̲o̲r̲t̲a̲n̲̲y̲ ̲e̲v̲e̲n̲t̲s ▶ ▶

NAME	DATE	EVENT

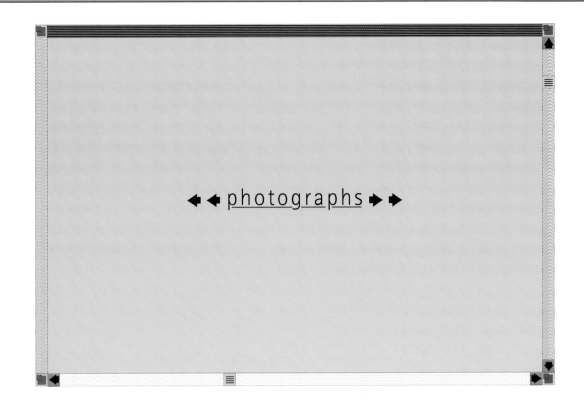

photographs

Were any people known to the family involved in the Gulf War, or other major events of the decade?

What do you think the 'nineties will be most remembered for in thirty years time?

2000 and BEYOND

How do you plan to celebrate the arrival of the new millenium?

What are your hopes for the family, the nation and the world in the twenty-first century?

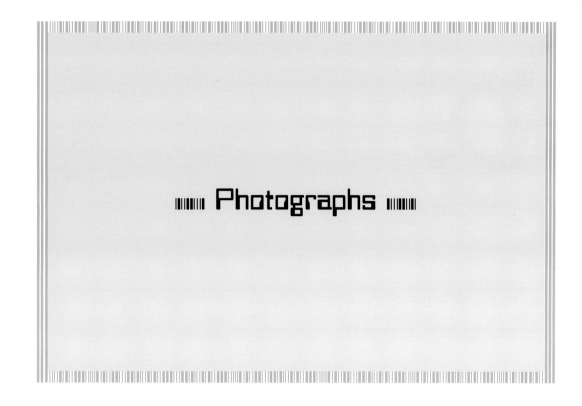

Photographs

Note below, as they occur, the family, national and international events you think future members of the family will regard as having been significant.

FAMILY EVENTS	NATIONAL EVENTS	INTERNATIONAL EVENTS

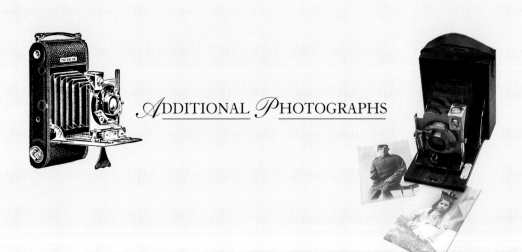

ADDITIONAL PHOTOGRAPHS